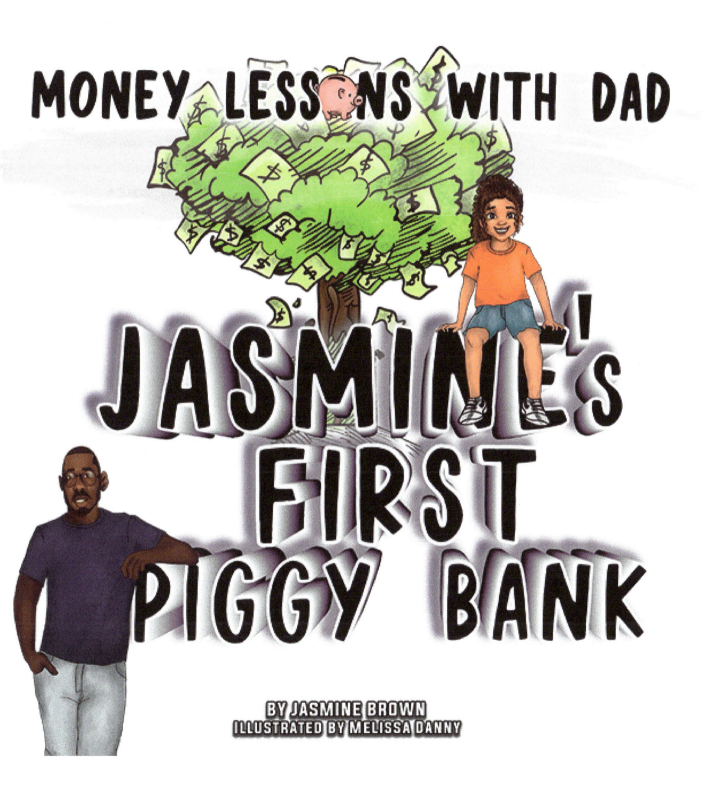

Disclaimer

The material contained in this book is intended for informational and educational purposes and will increase financial awareness. It is not intended for legal, accounting, or financial advice. You are responsible for your own investments and financial decisions at your own discretion. Readers are encouraged to seek professional advice to make informed financial decisions.

The author is not responsible or liable for any financial gains or losses of any kind arising on account of any action taken pursuant to the interpretation of this book.

All rights reserved. Printed in the United States of America.

Purchase of this book confirms you agree not to copy, distribute, or modify the content without the author's express written consent. Reproduction, redistribution, use, and transmission of any information contained in this book is strictly prohibited.
No part of this book may be used or reproduced in any manner whatsoever without written permission, except in the case of brief quotations in articles or reviews, which must be credited.

Copyright © 2022
ISBN: 978-1-7342662-5-2
Cover design by Melissa Danny
Character Illustrations by Melissa Danny
Book Editing by Vianka Cotton & Vickie Couch

Connect with Jasmine:
Instagram: @jasminetheauthor | @_factsforyouth
Twitter: @jastheauthor | @_factsforyouth
Facebook: @TheAuthorJasmineBrown | @factsforyouthnc
Email: info@jasminetheauthor.com
Website: www.jasminetheauthor.com

Hi! My name is Jasmine and this is my dad, Rodney! He's a financial advisor. I'm not sure what that means but he's like a doctor for people's money!

He talks to me about money all the time, but mostly when he says I can't get a toy I want! His favorite line is money doesn't grow on trees!

But wouldn't that be nice!

Today, he's giving me a money lesson! I'm only 7, but he says it's important for me to learn early.

"Ok Jasmine, today's lesson is save or spend!" he says as he hands me a box with a big yellow bow on top.

My eyes widen with excitement, then turn to wonder. It's not Christmas and it's definitely not my birthday! What could it be?

I rip off the bow and tear through the wrapping paper.

A pig?! What is this for? My favorite animal is an elephant, not a pig. They are smelly and muddy! Yuck!

I try to hide my frown from my dad, but he can tell that something is wrong. "It's a piggy bank!" he said.

"A piggy bank?" I ask.

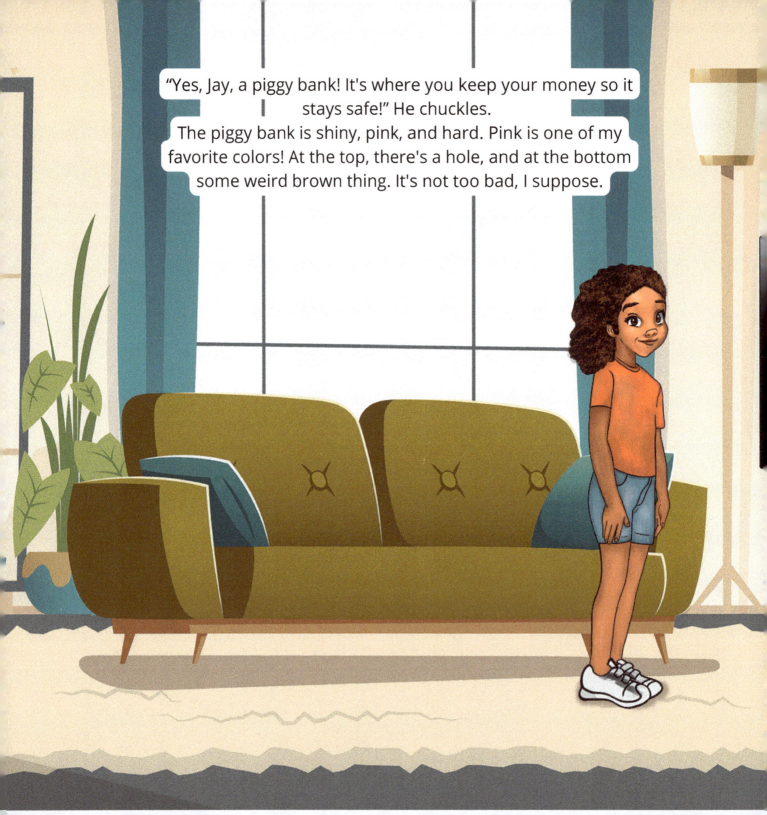

"Let's start your money lesson, your first task is to find all the loose change around the house! Then, deposit what you find in the piggy bank."

I already know mom puts loose change in the junk drawer in the kitchen. I'm going to find all the change in the world! I'm going to find so much money that I'm going to buy an elephant.

I grab my pig and run to the living room. First, I searched under the couch cushions.

Then my brother's messy room.

Finally, my parent's car! I bet I'll find 100 dollars! Wait, maybe I'll even find 500 hundred dollars.

Look! Pennies, quarters, dimes, and more all around the house. I even find my headphones I thought I lost and my favorite crayons.

Pretty soon my piggy bank will be overflowing! When I shake it, it goes clank clank clank!

"Jay, are you almost done?" My dad asks from the kitchen.
I run up to my dad, with a smile ear to ear. "Dad, feel how heavy this thing is!"

"Whoa!!! That is heavy!" My dad smiles, "Are you ready for your next task?"

"Yes! What is it?" I put the piggy bank on the coffee table. "It's time to count it up," he says. I take off the cork and change spills out.

"Do you see how much change I found daddy!?"

"Wow, that is a lot, Jay. Do you remember how much each coin is worth?"

"I sure do!"

This is a penny; it is worth one cent.

This is a nickel; it is worth 5 cents or 5 pennies.

This is a dime; it is worth 10 cents or 10 pennies.

This is a quarter; it is worth 25 cents or 25 pennies.

1 whole dollar is 4 quarters or 100 pennies.

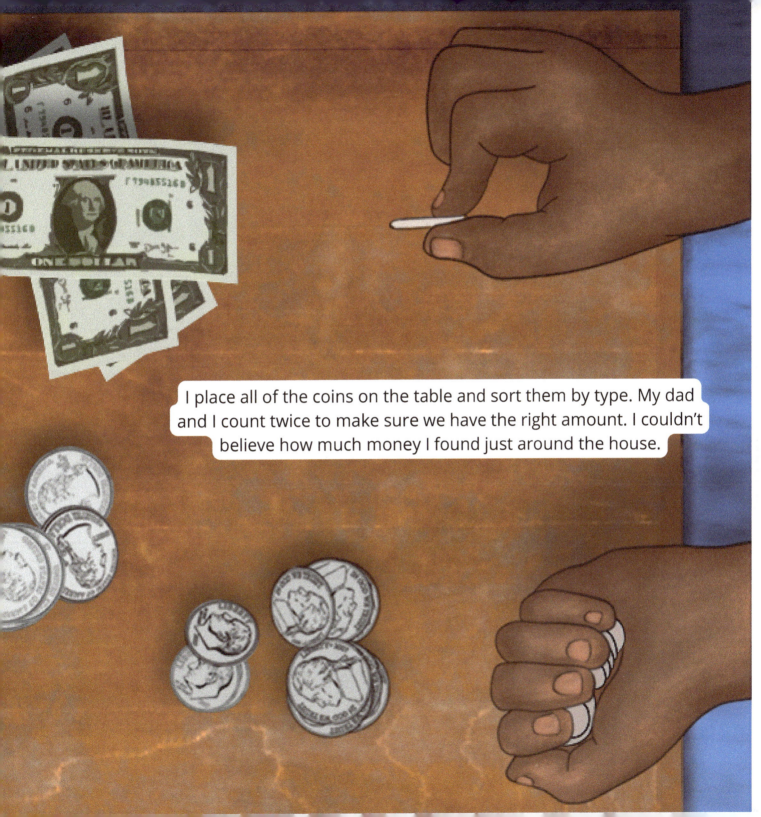

"Wow!" I say aloud. $3.46! I found so much! My dad hands me a dollar for doing so well. Now I have $4.46. I jump up and hug my dad. He kisses me on the cheek. I can't believe I have four whole dollars and forty-six cents! I can't wait to tell mommy. If I help with the dishes tonight, she may give me a quarter.

"So, Jay, what are you going to do with the money you found?"

"Is this enough to buy an elephant?" I ask.

My dad throws his head back and laughs, "No, not quite."

"Ahhh man...."

"Jay, you have two options, he says, with his most serious face. You can spend it or save it."

I've seen him hand money to the cashier at the grocery store before.

And when we went back to school shopping, he gave the clerk money for our clothes and shoes.

I ask my dad if that's what it means to spend.

He says I'm spot on!

"But what about saving, what is that?"

"Well Jasmine, saving money is the opposite of spending it."

"Like putting it back in the piggy bank?"

"Exactly."

"I could buy a small stuffed elephant from the Dollar store today or I can save my money for a long time and buy a real elephant!"

"A real elephant is a lot of money, Jasmine!"

"I know dad, but maybe I can keep searching around the house for more loose change, or sweep the floor for mommy!"

I decide that I'm going to save.

My dad smiles really big!

"Dad, do you save?"

"I sure do, all the time! And thanks to you guys, I spend all the time too!"

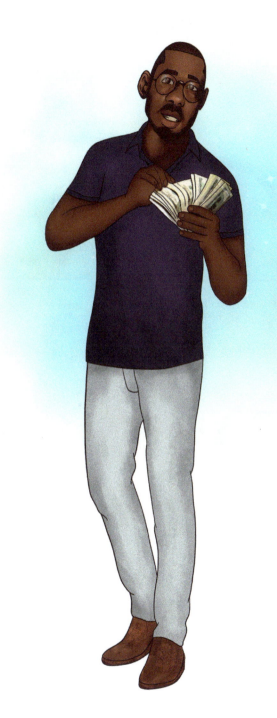

"Where is your piggy bank then?"

"I put my money in a bank account to be safe; a piggy bank won't hold all of my savings, but I had a piggy bank when I was younger just like you!"

"I want to save a lot too! I want a bank account!"

"Alright, I'll tell you what, keep saving and when you reach $50, we'll get you a bank account so you can save like me!"

I am giddy with anticipation!

I love my new piggy bank and I had a great time learning about saving and spending! Can't wait for my next money lesson with dad!

# Meet Jasmine and Rodney

Rodney Brown is a former Division I athlete, husband, and father of 5. He's been an expert in the finance field for over 25 years as a financial advisor for professional athletes. Following in her dad's footsteps, Jasmine Brown received her Bachelor's from NC State in Business and Finance and went on to start FACTS for Youth, a local nonprofit dedicated to equipping and empowering students with the ability to achieve financial freedom through early learning. In 2020, Jasmine also released her first book, The Money Club: A Teenage Guide to Financial Literacy. Rodney taught Jasmine important finance topics as a young girl, now, the daddy daughter duo, have teamed up to bring you Money Lessons with Dad to help others teach the child in their life.

CPSIA information can be obtained
at www.ICGtesting.com
Printed in the USA
BVHW021656050722
641354BV00005B/54